Father Michael McGivney

A Priest, a Leader

ÉDITIONS DU SIGNE

Father Michael McGivney

—

A Priest, a Leader

Written by
Mary-Cabrini Durkin

Illustrated by
Elisabetta Ferrero and Rita Ammassari

Special thanks to:

Carl A. Anderson, *Supreme Knight of the Knights of Columbus*
Father Gabriel O'Donnell, OP, *Vice-Postulator for the Cause of Canonization of Father McGivney*
Andrew Walther, *Vice President for Communications and Media*
Susan Brosnan, *Archivist*
Michèle Nuzzo-Naglieri, *Editorial and Research Specialist*

Illustrations
Elisabetta Ferrero, M.I.A.
Rita Ammassari, M.I.A.

Layout
Éditions du Signe

Publisher
Éditions du Signe
1, rue Alfred Kastler
B.P. 94 – 67038 Strasbourg Cedex 2
France
Tel (33) 3 88 78 91 91
Fax (33) 3 88 78 91 99
www.editionsdusigne.fr
info@editionsdusigne.fr

Meet Michael McGivney!

He loved his family, and they could always depend on him.

He enjoyed sports—especially baseball!

As a parish priest, he showed God's love to everyone.

He was a leader, who started the Knights of Columbus
to help men care for their families.

People liked being with Michael.

You will too.

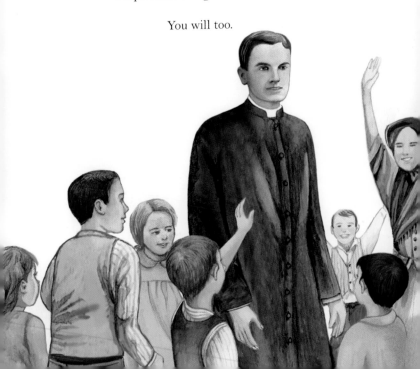

What makes a man a man?
What makes him a hero?
A leader? A saint?

For answers, meet Michael McGivney.

A man? He took responsibility for his family.
He faced challenges with courage.

A hero? He was quiet but strong.
He accomplished something great: founding
the Knights of Columbus, an international society
that has helped countless people.

A leader? He brought out the best in people.
He showed them how to use their talents.
He brought them together to work for a goal.

A saint? He dedicated himself to God.
He was kind to everyone and helped
others come closer to Christ.

He did all of this as a parish priest.

Thomaston

Cromwell

Waterbury   Meriden   Middletown

Wallingford

New Haven

"Michael, watch your little sisters. I'm depending on you."
"All right, Mother," Michael answered.
"Come on, Maryann. Come on, Rose.
Let's help Dad in the vegetable garden."
Michael was the oldest of seven brothers and sisters
in the lively McGivney household.
His birthday was August 12, 1852.
"Dad, when we finish weeding, will you toss
a few balls with me?" Michael asked.
"Sure, Michael. You'll be a good athlete."

8

Later the Lawlor family walked
across the bridge.
Michael was glad to see Martin.
"Hey Martin!
Let's race to the railroad track."
"You boys stay off that track,"
said both mothers at the same time.

The parents watched their children play.
"How long have you been in America?"
Mr. McGivney asked.
"We came from Ireland just three years ago,"
Mr. Lawlor answered. *"When did you come?"*
*"My wife and I both sailed from Ireland in 1849,
and we met here in Connecticut,"* said Michael's father.
"We're bringing our children up to be good Americans."

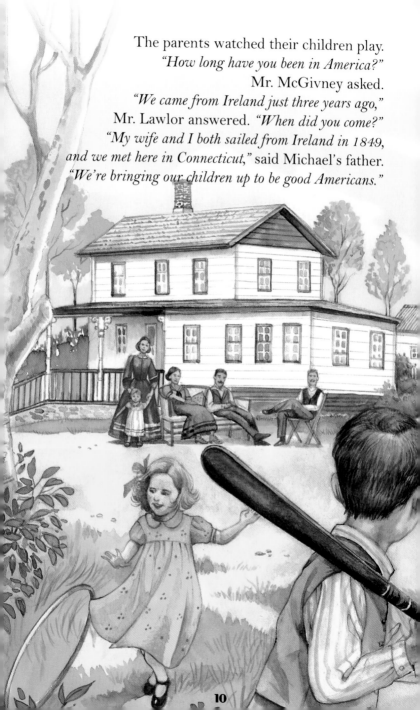

"Some Americans don't like us immigrants, do they?"
Mrs. Lawlor seemed sad. *"They look down on us."*
"It's hard for our kids to get a good education,"
her husband added.
"Father Hendricken is helping," said Michael's mother.
"He started a school in the old church basement.
Our parish just built our new Immaculate
Conception Church."

Mrs. McGivney was teaching her children at home, so that they would be ready for school.

"What does that spell?"

"Rabbit!" Michael answered.

"That's right. What you like to chase! Now copy these words onto your slate."

"Momma! Momma!" Maryann wanted to show what she knew, too. *"2 and 3 make 5!"*

"How old are you, Michael?
asked Mr. Thomas Meagher, the principal.
"I'm six, sir," said Michael.
"He knows enough to skip the first and second grades,"
said Mr. Meagher. "Mrs. McGivney, we're going to start
Michael in the third grade.
We'll see whether he can keep up with the other children."

Michael liked English class, especially reading stories.
"Math is harder for me," he thought.
Sometimes there were class plays.
*"Children, on Parents' Night you will perform
a play about Columbus coming to America,"*
announced Miss O'Connor.
"Who gets to be Columbus, Miss O'Connor?
asked Nora.
"Dennis will be Christopher Columbus,"
the teacher answered. *"Nora, you will be Queen Isabella.
Michael, you will be a sailor."*

Father Thomas Hendricken cared about all the families in his parish. He started the school so that the children would learn their faith. He visited the sick. Father Hendricken taught the boys to be altar servers. *"Michael, you seem to like serving Mass,"* he said one day. *"Why?"*

"At Mass I feel so close to God," Michael answered.
"When I grow up, I want to be a priest, like you, Father."
Father Hendricken thought for a while. At last he said,
"Pray, Michael. Ask the Holy Spirit to show you how to
serve God, and how to serve other people, too."

"*I'm so proud of you!*" Mrs. McGivney patted the collar
on Michael's graduation suit. He was thirteen,
and he was ready to graduate from East Main Street
School. After graduation, Michael got a job in
a spoon-making factory. He helped his parents
support the younger children.
For three years he worked in the factory,
and for three years he prayed, "*Jesus, please show
me how to follow you.*" He still hoped to become a priest.

"I want to be a priest,"
Michael told his parents when he was sixteen.
"Maybe God really is calling you,"
Mr. McGivney agreed.
Michael's parents planned how they would
save money for his tuition at the seminary.
In September, Michael and ten other young men from
Waterbury rode the train to Canada,
to St. Hyacinthe Seminary.

At the seminary, young men were preparing to be priests. Michael studied hard. *"Hey Mike! It's time for lunch,"* a classmate called to him. *"Coming!"* Michael answered. *"That math is tough."* *"But you won a prize in English,"* his friend said. Michael laughed. *"I have to work a lot harder at algebra."*

Michael still liked baseball.
He played left field for the seminary's
Charter Oaks team.
"Run, Mike, run!" yelled John Splain
as Michael crossed home plate.
"That's his third run scored," cheered Dick O'Grady.
"A win for the Charter Oaks!"

When Michael was 20, his father died suddenly. Michael rushed home to Waterbury to care for his family. What would they do without Mr. McGivney's salary?

"Rose and I have jobs," Maryann explained. *"We can support Mother and the little ones."*

"But we can't afford seminary tuition anymore," Michael said. He got a job in Waterbury.

But soon a letter arrived from the bishop.
Michael would receive a scholarship
to St. Mary's Seminary in Baltimore, Maryland.
For four more years, he studied
and prepared to become a good priest.

Michael was ordained by
Archbishop James Gibbons
on December 22, 1877.
Now he was a priest.

What a happy Christmas
that was for the McGivney family!
Father Michael offered his first Mass
in his home parish,
Immaculate Conception in Waterbury.

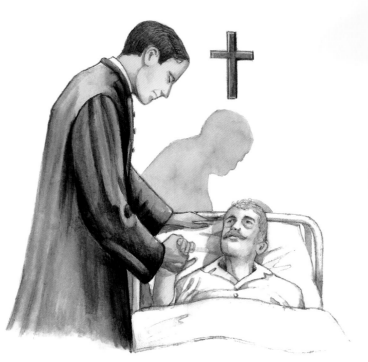

Soon Father Michael was sent to St. Mary's Parish
in New Haven. He helped the pastor, Father
Patrick Murphy, who was sick.
When Father Murphy died a year later,
Father Patrick Lawlor became the pastor.
Father Michael offered Mass every day.
In Confession, he shared God's
forgiveness for people's sins.
He visited sick people
to comfort them.

The parish picnic was the biggest event of every summer. Father Michael organized the activities. The children held races and rode ponies. Everyone tried to win prizes at the game booths and raffles. And, of course, there were baseball games.

Father Michael liked teaching religion.
He had the children act out Gospel stories.
He helped the teenagers run their clubs
and put on plays and picnics.
"It's fun with Father McGivney around,"
they agreed.
He suggested that the women sell coffee
and desserts to help pay off the parish debt
— $164,000.

The young men's club put on comedies like
Handy Andy and sold tickets to raise funds.
"They're having a good time and helping others,"
Father Michael thought.
 *"If they spent all their time in bars,
 they would be getting into trouble."*
He invited more young men to join.

Some did get drunk and even committed crimes.
Father Michael visited them in jail.
"God will forgive you," he said,
"and God will help you to lead a better life."
One prisoner was Chip Smith. While he was drunk,
he killed a policeman. Chip was sentenced to death.
Father Michael and Sisters of Mercy visited Chip
and told him about God.

Before his execution, Chip asked pardon for his crime.
He said, *"I have asked God to forgive me,
and I believe that I shall die a happy death."*
Father Michael stayed with him until the end,
and he comforted Chip's mother and sister.

Father Michael visited the Downes family
when their father Edward died suddenly.
His wife Catherine and their eight
children had no money.
"How can I keep my family together?"
Mrs. Downes sobbed. *"Our relatives can help a little.
But the judge will take Alfred away from me."*

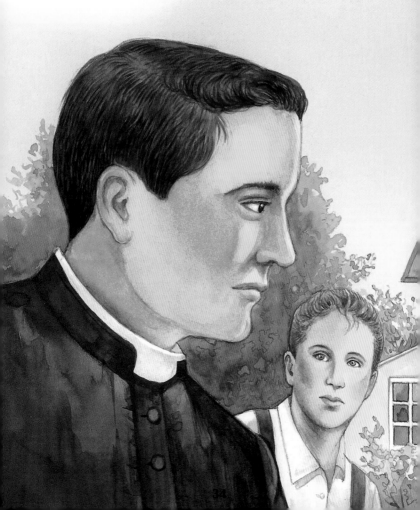

Father Michael thought and prayed.
He asked Mr. Patrick McKiernan
to help him take responsibility for Alfred.
In the courtroom a few weeks later, the judge asked,
*"Will anyone take care of this young fellow,
Alfred Downes?"*
Father Michael stood up. *"I will,"* he said.
With Father Michael as his guardian,
and with Mr. McKiernan's help,
Alfred could live with his family.

Father Michael preached good sermons.
Even non-Catholics like Alida Harwood came to listen.
Alida became a Catholic.
Her father, Dr. Harwood, was angry.
When Alida was sick, she begged her father
to let Father Michael come to pray with her.
Dr. Harwood would not allow it.

After Alida died, he finally met Father Michael. He saw how kind this priest was. Father Michael comforted Alida's parents, and they allowed him to offer Catholic funeral prayers for Alida.

Men's clubs were popular in New Haven.
They had secret passwords and ceremonies
and fancy uniforms. There were many societies:
the Foresters, the Modern Woodmen of America,
the Masons, the Red Knights, and others.
Their members felt like brothers.

Some societies saved money for life insurance.
If a member died, his "brothers" would help his family
with the money they needed. Joining a society like this
was one way for men to take care of their families.

Father Michael thought about Alfred's family.
He remembered his own father's death.
Men often died of injuries from their work,
and most diseases had no medical remedies.
*"When a husband and father dies, his widow and orphans
have a very hard time. What can be done to help them?"*

At the time, secret societies were prohibited by the Church. Father Michael worried that Catholic men might leave their faith in order to join these groups. He wanted to start a society for Catholic men. *"They will be like brothers, helping their families and growing in their faith,"* he told his friends.

Father Michael invited the Catholic men
of New Haven to meet in Saint Mary's
basement in October 1881.
Eighty men came. Twelve volunteered
to plan with Father Michael.
"We'll call ourselves the Knights of Columbus,"
they agreed.

Christopher Columbus was the heroic Italian Catholic
who had sailed to America in 1492.
Father Michael and the other men explained
the new group to Bishop Lawrence McMahon.
Even though a priest had begun
the Knights of Columbus,
lay men would run it. The bishop approved.

Father Michael McGivney worked hard
to reach his goals. He never gave up.
Nothing could stop him.
The Knights of Columbus
faced problems.

Even though the State of Connecticut recognized
them in March 1882, their membership grew slowly.
Some of the leaders argued with each other.
"'Unity, charity' is our motto,"
Father Michael reminded them.

Others wanted to quit.
"Families need the Knights," Father Michael insisted.
"Many widows don't have enough to feed their little ones.
Poor children go hungry. They even die."

Then a surprising letter came from the town of Meriden. Men wanted a council (local group) of the Knights of Columbus there. This good idea was spreading!

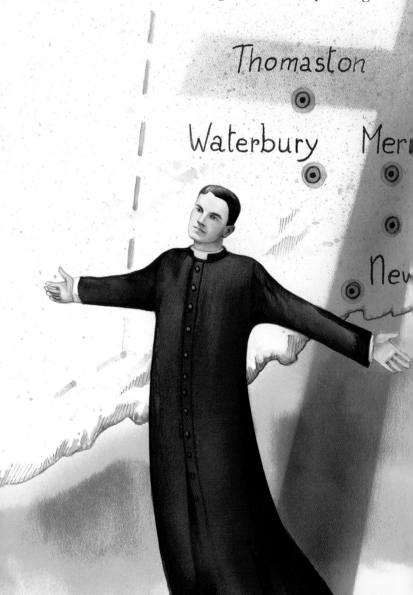

Thomaston

Waterbury

Mer

Nev

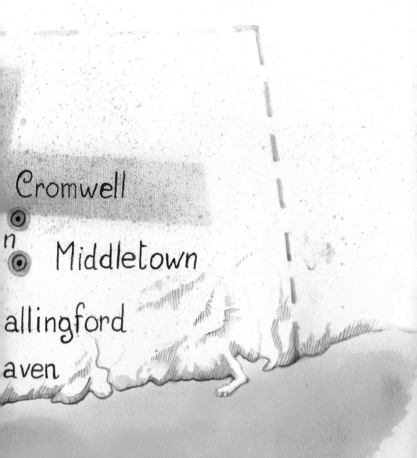

Cromwell

n

Middletown

allingford

aven

Other towns started councils, too: Middletown,
Wallingford, Cromwell, and Portland. They held their
first annual convention in 1883 and by May 1884,
there were nearly 400 members. Father Michael saw
that the Knights had good leaders. He resigned
as secretary. *"I will be your chaplain,"* he told them,
"but I must concentrate on my parish."
Hundreds of Knights held a grand parade
in New Haven in 1885.

"Your next assignment is to be the pastor of Saint Thomas Parish in Thomaston," said a letter from the bishop. The people of Saint Mary's cried as Father Michael said goodbye.

"He's been kind to everyone," said one parishioner.

"He's worked so hard for us!" said another.

Father Michael loved his parishioners
in Thomaston, too. Young people
knew he was their friend.
He helped the Christian Doctrine Society
raise money for the parish library by
directing an old favorite, the comedy
Handy Andy.
His Sunday school classes put
on a big Thanksgiving show.

Father Michael had to take care of the parish in Terryville, too. That meant traveling back and forth in a horse-drawn buggy up and down hilly roads, even in rain and snow.

The McGivneys were glad that Thomaston was close to Waterbury. Father Michael visited his family often. He encouraged his brothers John and Patrick to study hard. They both wanted to be priests like him. His sister Annie led the choir at Saint Thomas. When their mother died, Father Michael offered her funeral Mass. He was very sad.

The Knights of Columbus had grown to over
4,000 members in Connecticut by 1888.
Men in Providence, Rhode Island, wanted
to start a council. Would their bishop approve?
They invited Father Michael to talk with him in 1888.
Father Michael convinced Bishop Matthew Harkins
to approve the Knights. Now the Knights of Columbus
were becoming a national organization.

In one more year they grew to over 6,000 members. Their founder, Father Michael McGivney, was their Supreme Chaplain.

He was happy to know that many families had recieved support.

Father Michael worked very hard.
There was no time to rest. His health grew weak.
When he caught the flu, he could not get well.
On Father Michael's thirty-eighth birthday,
he stayed in bed. He was dying.
As a priest, he had visited many sick people.
He had helped them prepare for death.
Now it was Father Michael's turn.
His heart was peaceful.
He had one request:
"Bury me with my parents."
He had one wish:
*"I only wish I could see John
and Patrick ordained priests."*
On August 14, 1890,
Father Michael McGivney
went to heaven.

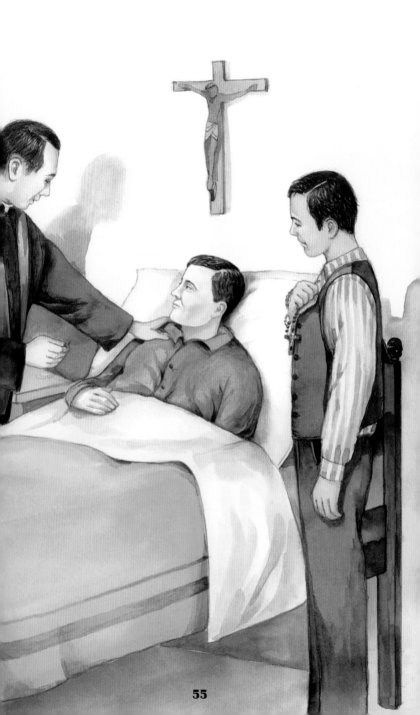

So many people came to Father Michael's funeral that
Saint Thomas Church could not hold them.
They filled the church and the front lawn.
A huge cross made of flowers honored him
as the founder and chaplain of the Knights
of Columbus.

The Knights of Columbus have spread to many countries. In more than 125 years, millions have participated in their mission: to help men care for their families. Spiritual programs such as prayer and attending Mass together strengthen their Catholic faith. The Knights have saved countless people from poverty and even death. They feed the hungry, help the weak, rebuild homes, and restore churches. After they die, life insurance programs assist their families. Father McGivney's spirit of unity, charity, and brotherhood is still the ideal of the Knights of Columbus. The Knights have added patriotism to this list.

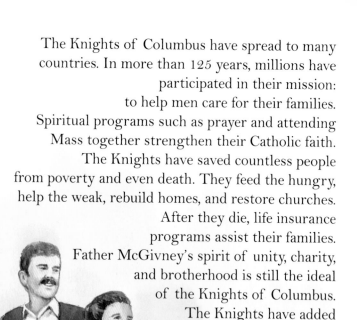

Father Michael McGivney was holy, which means he loved and served God and others very, very much. Founding the Knights of Columbus was important. Serving God's people is even more important. Maybe someday the Catholic Church will honor him as a saint. In 1997, careful research about his life began. He is now called "Venerable," meaning worthy of honor. Many people pray for blessings, asking Venerable Michael McGivney to join them in praying. Some pray for a miracle, such as a cure from sickness.

Scientists and doctors must study a cure to discover whether it has natural causes or not.

If God grants a miracle through Father Michael's intercession, he will be called "Blessed,"
which means happy in heaven.

If there is a second miracle, a person is called "Saint."
The saints are our heavenly friends and models
of how to live.

Father Michael McGivney is a model
of the spiritual greatness of a parish priest.

Dear Father in heaven,

Thank you for the many gifts you give us each day,

and for your loving care for those in need.

Thank you for giving us Father Michael McGivney

as a living example of faith and love.

His life and work show us your fatherly care,

the love of Jesus on the cross,

and the power of the Holy Spirit in our lives.

Help us to become more like

Father McGivney in serving others.

We ask this through Jesus Christ, your Son.

Amen.

If you would like to know more about

Father Michael McGivney,

you can visit

www.fathermcgivney.org

———

To learn more about

the **Knights of Columbus,**

you can visit

www.kofc.org

Or write to

Knights of Columbus

One Columbus Plaza

New Haven, CT 06510

U.S.A.